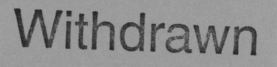

Out and About at the GREENHOUSE

by Bitsy Kemper
illustrated by Zachary Trover

Special thanks to our advisers for their expertise:

Tim Metcalf, Greenhouse Director
University of California, Davis Botanical Conservatory

Susan Kesselring, M.A., Literacy Educator
Rosemount–Apple Valley–Eagan (Minnesota) School District

PICTURE WINDOW BOOKS
Minneapolis, Minnesota

To the Carluccio family, thanks for growing Vince!—BK

Editor: Nick Healy
Designer: Tracy Kaehler
Page Production: Lori Bye
Creative Director: Keith Griffin
Editorial Director: Carol Jones
The illustrations in this book were created digitally.

Picture Window Books
5115 Excelsior Boulevard
Suite 232
Minneapolis, MN 55416
877-845-8392
www.picturewindowbooks.com

Printed in the United States of America.

Library of Congress Cataloging-in-Publication Data
Kemper, Bitsy.
Out and about at the greenhouse / by Bitsy Kemper ; illustrated by Zachary Trover.
p. cm. — (Field trips)
Includes bibliographical references.
ISBN-13: 978-1-4048-2279-5 (hardcover)
ISBN-10: 1-4048-2279-8 (hardcover)
1. Greenhouses—Juvenile literature. I. Trover, Zachary, ill. II. Title. III. Field trips
(Picture Window Books)
SB415.K36 2007
631.5'83—dc22   2006003525

We're going on a field trip to a greenhouse.
We can't wait!

Things to find out:

What is a greenhouse?

What grows there?

What keeps it warm inside?

Why do we need greenhouses?

Welcome to Uncle Pat's Plants. My name is Vince. I'm a horticulturist. A horticulturist is someone who knows a lot about plants. Has anyone visited a greenhouse like this before?

Some greenhouses grow fruits and vegetables, and some grow other plants. At Uncle Pat's, we grow ornamentals. That is a fancy name for pretty plants and flowers. We sell these ornamentals all year long.

Outdoors, most of these plants will grow only in spring or summer. In a greenhouse, we can grow our plants anytime, even when it's cold outside.

A horticulturist makes sure plants bloom and grow. He or she figures out the best temperature, the right amount of water, and which plant food is best. A horticulturist is like a plant doctor.

5

We'll start the tour in our shop. This is where some of our customers buy our flowers and plants.

Ann is pruning plants to make them look nice. She snips off dead leaves, wipes away dust, and checks for bugs. People like buying plants they wouldn't be able to grow on their own. We sell lots of flowers during the winter.

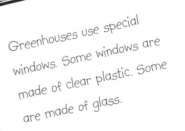

Greenhouses use special windows. Some windows are made of clear plastic. Some are made of glass.

Once you're inside, it's easy to see why plants like the greenhouse. It's nice and warm in here. There are windows everywhere. The glass lets the sun's warmth through and holds it inside.

A greenhouse uses heat from the sun, which is called solar energy. Our plants need warm air to grow. On sunny days like today, our greenhouse collects solar energy and stores it. The air inside the greenhouse stays warm even when it's cold and gray outside.

This poster shows how the greenhouse works. Rays of sunlight come in through the windows. The plants and soil inside the greenhouse absorb the heat from the sun. Then they give off heat at night, when the sunlight is gone.

Some greenhouses use gas or electric heaters to help keep them warm during the cold season. Others use only solar energy.

Different plants have different needs. Plants from the desert like dry air. Plants from the tropics like damp air. Our greenhouse has different rooms to please different sorts of plants.

We keep this room very damp. The air is so wet that it almost feels like it's raining in here. Can you tell it's also a little cooler? This part of the greenhouse faces east. It gets morning sunlight.

Take a deep breath. You'll notice how this room smells like a forest. The plants that grow best here are ferns and begonias. We also have insect-eating plants like the Venus flytrap. Don't touch that one! It might snap shut on your finger.

Some plants need lots of water to grow properly. Warm and humid air holds more water than cold air does. Warm, wet air makes water-hungry plants happy.

This room gets afternoon sun. The air is hot and dry in here. Cacti and other desert plants love this weather. This room is a little bigger than the other ones. We need more room to walk around the plants so we don't get poked by the cactus needles.

Tim is replanting a cactus. It grew so much that it needs a bigger pot.

Greenhouses have plants of many sizes. The plants start as tiny seedlings. They are cared for so they will grow until they are sold.

Some important parts of the greenhouse are overhead. The roof has vents, or openings, that we can open and close. Sometimes it gets too hot in here. When that happens, I open the vents. That lets out hot air, which always rises.

You can also see lots of lights up there. The lightbulbs are special. They are called high-intensity lights. That means they give off a lot of light. Each bulb is as bright as 16 of the bulbs you would use in a lamp at home.

These special lights act like the sun on cloudy days. Light is like food to plants. It helps them live and grow.

Lights with HID, or High Intensity Discharge, are more efficient than the fluorescent bulbs in homes and schools. They let off more light but use less electricity. They cost less to use and help save energy.

You probably know how important water is to plants. All plants need at least a little bit of water. Some plants need a lot. Every type of plant is different. What works for a lily won't work for a cactus.

FERTILIZER

Our greenhouse has sprinklers that water the plants. The water turns on and off automatically. The system is a great help, but each plant still needs careful attention from one of us.

We check the plants several times a week. Two plants might not grow the same way. One plant might need a little extra fertilizer. Another one might not.

Fertilizer is like vitamins and minerals for plants. It gives plants some of what they need to grow. Greenhouse workers use fertilizer only when needed. Too much of it can hurt the plants and soil.

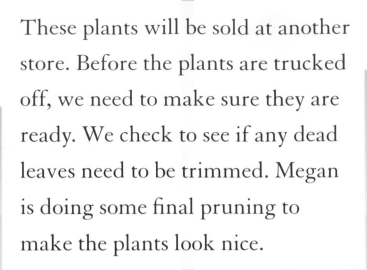

These plants will be sold at another store. Before the plants are trucked off, we need to make sure they are ready. We check to see if any dead leaves need to be trimmed. Megan is doing some final pruning to make the plants look nice.

LOADING

TDK 422

Once loaded onto the truck, the plants are hauled to a big warehouse. The company that buys the plants will give each one a label. From there, the plants are sent to stores, where customers can pick the ones they want.

We want customers to be happy with what they buy. We pay special attention to our plants so they will grow up healthy and beautiful.

Ornamental plants are the most common type of plant grown in greenhouses. Vegetables come in second.

This is the end of our tour. Remember, greenhouses are important. Without them, we wouldn't have some of our favorite plants.

I hope you enjoyed the greenhouse. Everyone gets to take home a plant. Make sure it gets lots of sunlight and water. Thanks for coming!

TRAP THE HEAT

What you need:
2 identical glass jars
4 cups (1 liter) of cold water
10 ice cubes
1 clear plastic bag
1 rubber band
a thermometer
a notepad and pencil

What you do:

1. Fill each jar with 2 cups (0.5 L) of cold water. Measure the temperature of the water in each jar; it should be the same. Write down the time and water temperature. Add five ice cubes to each jar.

2. Cover the top of one jar with a plastic bag; secure the bag with a rubber band. Leave the other jar open. Set the jars on a sunny windowsill for 30 minutes. Measure the temperature of the water in each jar. Note the time and temperatures each time you check.

3. Leave the jars in the sunlight for an afternoon, and measure the temperatures occasionally. At the end of the day, check the temperature of the water in each jar one more time.

4. Check your results. Did covering the top of one jar affect the water's temperature?

FUN FACTS

- Do you want to be a gardener when you grow up? Study hard! Professional gardeners and horticulturists need to understand subjects like chemistry, biology, art, and mathematics.

- Clean windows capture the warmth of the sun better than dirty ones. Greenhouse workers regularly wash the windows, inside and out, to keep sunlight streaming in.

- Poppies are flowers that people have grown for thousands of years. Remains of poppies have been found in Egyptian tombs dating back 3,000 years.

- The greenhouse effect is when sun-warmed air can't escape. Earth's atmosphere has a natural, and important, greenhouse effect. It keeps our planet warm. But many scientists are concerned that pollution is changing Earth's natural greenhouse effect. They are concerned that our planet could get too warm.

- People who are good with plants are said to have a "green thumb."

GLOSSARY

fertilizer—a material added to soil to help plants grow

horticulturist—an expert in growing plants

humid—moist

ornamentals—plants grown and used for decoration

prune—to trim or remove branches to shape a plant or help its growth

solar energy—heat made by the sun

tropics—a warm region of Earth that is near the equator

TO LEARN MORE

At the Library

Greenstein, Elaine. *One Little Seed*. New York: Viking, 2004.

Richardson, Joy. *Flowers*. Milwaukee: Gareth Stevens Publishing, 2005.

Star, Fleur. *Plant*. New York: DK Publishing, 2005.

Winckler, Suzanne. *Planting the Seed: A Guide to Gardening*. Minneapolis: Lerner Publications, 2002.

On the Web

FactHound offers a safe, fun way to find Internet sites related to this book. All of the sites on FactHound have been researched by our staff.

1. Visit *www.facthound.com*
2. Type in this special code for age-appropriate sites: 1404822798
3. Click on the FETCH IT button.

Your trusty FactHound will fetch the best sites for you!

INDEX

24

Look for all of the books in the Field Trips series: